# Nothing Personal

*Poems*

## Sibyl Ruth

IRON
PRESS

# Sibyl Ruth

SIBYL RUTH grew up in Manchester and now lives in the West Midlands. She started writing poetry when a long viral illness, ME, made it impossible for her to do much else. In the past she has been a cook in a vegetarian restaurant and a gardener in a graveyard, but she currently works for the Citizens Advice Bureau.

*Photograph by Barbara Jones*

First published 1995 by IRON Press
5 Marden Terrace, Cullercoats
North Shields, Northumberland NE30 4PD
Tel: 091 - 253 1901

Typeset by David Stephenson
in Times 10 point

Book design by Peter Mortimer

Printed by Peterson Printers, South Shields

ISBN  0 906228 52 2

Acknowledgements are due to the following magazines
in which some of the poems first appeared;
*Ambit, Distaff, Fatchance, Frogmore Papers,
Illuminations, IRON, The North, The Rialto,
Scratch, Smith's Knoll, Staple, Tears in the Fence.*

IRON Press books
are represented & distributed by
Password Books Ltd
23 New Mount Street
Manchester M4 4DE
Tel: 061 - 953 4009
Fax: 061 - 953 4001

# The Poems

# A Very Old T-shirt

Dad wouldn't unlock the door to me
that summer.  Mum was in hospital,

covered with tar and bandages.  Only my brother
was happy, pulling the dog's tail.

My boyfriend told me he was bisexual.
We went to a club where I danced

in slow circles with a woman.  She touched my hips.
He chatted up a bloke with bad teeth and nails.

We had sex because his best mate's parents
were in Marbella.  I'd been waiting

but when he burrowed into me, it made no difference.
There was a nightdress under the pillow

that didn't belong to me.  I fingered the nylon
over and over till I slept.

# Ten Years and Matilda

Too many occasions I've said my name
or you left your sentence after the tone.
If one of us does catch the other at home
our schedules rarely coincide.
Cancellations - a bout of cystitis,
that conference in Geneva - also kept us.

The wine bar we pick has been gutted,
refurbished as often as ourselves
since you were eighteen in green culottes
and I wore my grandma's fur coat.
Both of us used to be ravenous.
Now nothing tastes how we expected.

Round and round the plate
pursuing details of divorces
- who's gone in for therapy -
like a forkload of pasta.

Once strong fibres held us
tight as a trampoline.
We were enthusiasts, twin acrobats
who fell only to shoot up again.
These days each movement is careful,
knowing the fabric's half-perished,
might give under pressure,
almost fit to be thrown.

At St James's Park we lob
old slogans across the platform.
Opposite trains will arrive
any minute to digest us.

# Baby Love

The children I don't have
are crying out once more.
Everywhere I'm followed
by their hungry calls.

They reach through brick and plasterboard.

I nearly touch their hairy scalps,
almost have my finger gripped
by spider hands.

They mean to come inside my house
and sit there snug and warm,
drinking my drink,
eating my food.

Who do they think they are?

I can't make them let go,
this problem family, my brood
that can't be born.

# Bearing Up

Unwanted sun in the living room.
With a snap of the blind he cuts it
then sags to a chair, eyes closed,
rubbing out angry skin
where glasses nipped his nose.
After years of papers, publications,
he will be stopping
in the same office by the coffee machine,
disturbed by colleagues' laughter.
Every application has been passed over.


His wife hovers in the hallway.
*No, he hasn't got a headache.*
*Absolutely fine.* She is off
to bang saucepans in the kitchen.
He isn't about to leave her,
take the car from the garage,
drive to that reasonably priced motel
with en suite bath
and a view over the Beacons.
Too much has gone between them.


A knife cracks to the floor.
Nothing broken. All faces on him.
Under the table his hands are shaking.
One of the children.
They clutched his palm once,
asked him to do arithmetic.
Now they have grown huge feet
and use calculators.
Each evening spent on secret phone calls
or playing their harsh records.

Coffee and a paperback detective
keep him down after the late weather.
He tucks a blanket round the quilt.
Across the gap, her scraped breathing.
Yes, other men might well go
to the doctor, go off the rails,
walk off the pier's end with bills unpaid.
Not him.  He's built of stronger stuff.
He has made his bed and will carry on
as normal.  Bearing up.

# Today

By half eight
her neighbours are gone to their offices.

Houses abandoned
to rumpled beds and unwashed cornflake bowls.

Nobody calls.
She gets on with the chores.

Only when birdsong
fades out of the tree

and there's no traffic on the road
she imagines

into such moments
a bomb could fall.

Radio 4 redeems her.
She switches to its stories.

News headlines
tidy as a chest of drawers.

Disasters happen elsewhere.
Smooth voices reassure.

# Daughter

So where did she roll to,
my bright sixpence
of a girl?

Was it silly Mama
who left her for the dustbin men,
or dropped her in the loft
one rainy day?

More likely
it was those giggly girls
took her away.
She tiptoed back with smoke in her coat
and a stink of vinegar.

I've been shortchanged
getting this crosspatch,
all sharp edges,
accusations.

She comes after me
drumming her heels against my tidy cupboards.
I gave her food.
Now blood isn't enough.

# Two Minds

*Shame*, says my mother.
Like a song on a long-player,
sounding her warped note
of accusation.

Because I failed to bring her babies,
red-faced and moist
as geraniums.
She would only muddle their names.

I have driven a hundred miles
to tug weeds from her dark garden.
And to up-end a laundry bag
of intimate stains.

Now she follows me
round and round the kitchen.
Setting out tins I don't want,
washing implements before I use them.

*Tidy*, she states.
As I take hold
of a globe of old garlic
that crumples to paper in my hand.

More often her sentences falter
like party guests
in a doorway,
uncertain why they came.

The stairs deceive
and furniture puts on disguises.
Together they make her skin
into a livid canvas.

Her hands are birds.
They beat upwards, blunder.
I fill half a cup and add cold water.
*Nasty!* she cries.

Moon-faced she appears
in my room at night,
stares for a minute then goes.
*Tomorrow*, I tell the pillow.

# Bear

Bear is not in his box.
I run to Mum in the garden.
She is unpegging pillowcases
and grown-up underwear.

She says
*He was so disgusting*
*I just had to give him a bath.*
*Look up there!*

Something waving
from a blue nylon bag
that drips like a nosebleed
onto the crazy paving.

She says
*You're far too old*
*and it's not hygienic*
*to be carrying him everywhere.*

Mum has huge hands.
They rub shampoo in my eyes.
Drag the comb twice a day
through my hair.

When I was at school
she pushed Bear in the sink.
Held his head down
in the dangerous pool.

Tonight a new animal
sits on top of my pyjamas
stinking of soapflakes
and fresh air.

I throw him out of bed
and lie alone in the dark.
Mum did it alright.
She killed my Bear.

# Punishment

*Go to your room.*
*Up to your room and stay there.*

Dad shouts
shaking a high arm.
His head turned to red meat
and big as a cartoon.

*Sorry?*
*It's no good saying you're sorry.*

Mum smiles
as she smacks her iron down
on someone's flat underwear.
She doesn't want to interfere.

*Bad girl.*
That's what they both say.
*Rude child. Naughty.*
Tasting the words like sweeties.

*You know very well what you've done.*
*And don't stamp on the stairs...*

Her unbreakable Sindy doll waits
with five Blue Peter annuals
a smug alarm-clock and the bear.
No one can help.

Lucky she still fits inside the cupboard
set into the wall
where the dark is fuzzy as a blanket.
The pipes roar like on holiday.

She will sit here till teatime
quite happy
to pick at the skin of her hands.
Hurting herself.

# Coming On Nicely

Her parents' faces are balloons
she could puncture with one bad word.
But she lets Dad give her a tube of Smarties
every Saturday. Because he's sorry
he can't help any longer with her maths.
Mum brings home a dress labelled 'Junior Miss'.
It is mauve with big white spots on
and has to be taken back.

Parties turn risky.
All the long-haired boys in cowboy boots
tried their luck down the off-licence,
choosing apricot wine and cider.
Music spins. The lights get switched off.
Girls who have B-cup breasts and blue eyeshadow
wait their turn at spin the bottle.
Some do a lot more than kissing.

Only she is big-footed, flat, clumsy.
In sewing her French knots look ugly as pimples
near the place where her scissors caught the fabric.
The teacher goes spare, ripping her work up
before half the class. Across the corridor
the lads are busy making copper ashtrays.
She's going to be a doctor anyway.
It doesn't matter.

Her odd stomach ache twists during physics
and the first blood comes oozing, unstoppable.
Thighs clamped to the lab stool
she can't raise a hand, find excuses.
As people copy the experiment she estimates
how fast the stain will spread to her skirt.
Five minutes left. When she stands
the boys on the next bench are sure to notice.

# Short Measure

I want to pick up somebody my own size
and ask for trouble.

I want to dance my legs off and talk dirty,
to go swimming in deep water.

I want to poke my nose in, stir the pot,
stew in a slow oven, get my fingers burned.

I want to make a four course meal
and throw the dishes out of the kitchen window.

I want to play hide and seek,
and hunt the thimble.   .

I want to hit boundaries,
score perfect sixes.

I want the rub of the magic lamp,
the angel rushing down the unlit alley.

I want to come to my senses.

# Couple

**couple n.** *a pair of equal forces acting on the same body in opposite and parallel directions. - v.t. to join together. - v.i. to pair sexually.*

I can't stand here much longer.
My toes curled over the highboard's edge

while he dabs about, his strokes
disturbing the surface of the water.

I should fix my eyes on a point in front,
forget that big dip

when I belly-flopped,
got stung, smacked breathless.

This one beckons me off-balance.
*Take the plunge*, he says.

Then my arms extend
and my lungs unfurl like flags.

He has such a sleek head,
a seal's dark eyes.

Striking an attitude, I thrust.
Now there is nothing to control or touch

as I go up, catch time by the heels,
hang weightless, held by sheer air

above that amphibian,
unfathomable creature.

One moment's sweet inertia of the body
before I somersault

an arrow, a perfect swallow
flying headlong into his element.

# Sharing

She was a monetary convenience,
a four-year phase.  He never made a move
when they passed at night on the stair,
(kimono pulled fast against her titless chest).
Politely he'd flatten himself.

Closest he ever came
was picking tails of her sluttish hair
out of the basin.  Always they knocked first,
kept separate cupboards.
Their intimacy an irritation.

Phonecalls delayed by her monotonous recitals
and cackled laughter.
The way she blocked his path to the kettle.
That god-awful racket when she sang along
with Johnny Mathis.

And her finicking snacks of smelly cheese
on two cream crackers.
The kitchen fogged with smoke
from her roll-ups.
His newspaper folded to the women's page.

Then she got her own house
(he was invited once)
full of expensive whatnots.
*Egyptian sculpture,* she said. *Jardinières.*
He felt relief.

Able to afford the luxury
of spare rooms and tenantless evenings.
But now he finds himself
thinking of talks they didn't have.
It's like the start of a bank holiday.  Or grief.

# A Man's Place

*I live alone*, he said.
Only she can't see it.
His walls jostle with pictures of ancestors.
Black and white and button-eyed,
peering out at her
from their serious dead universe.

His twice-weekly daughters
are in the letters A to G,
penned in felt-tip on the piano keys.
Bold drawings taped to the refrigerator
bear wobbly first names.
*Yes, they were wanted. Both of them planned.*

While the wife lives divorced
in a convenient drawer
getting pulled out to prove a likeness.
A square-faced woman
whose chin tilts every trespasser
the same unworried smile.

*Make yourself at home*, was the invitation.
But how when he sits
eying her like a reckless purchase?
Does she not blend with the décor?
Even the two fat rabbits
round the back belong here more.

Music jumps from the bedroom
as she sets a toothbrush on edge,
ignores the curled lip of a carpet tile.
Her reflection whispering,
*Isn't this what you wanted?*
*Now stake your claim. Move in.*

# Promises Promises

You hold a glistering brochure,
fat packages of invitation;
with an offer to stand by,
help me take a break
from long-sleeved solitude,
who'd be left at the ticket barrier
flapping hands like an anxious parent.

Fast forwarding, I see
you and me slurred with wine.
My feet slap the cobbles of a fishing village.
Above us the constellations look different.
We shall sleep well
in our small white room
beneath a picture of the Blessed Virgin.

But bare single nights
at your place in Smethwick
or my Black Country flat are all we manage.
Other dates bring excuses, loopholes,
last-minute cancellations.
The best of each one already packed and gone
for some inland territory.

Now when milk sickens in the carton,
and a wasp beats tired wings
against its trap of honey
I want us to flip back through that catalogue
of easy blue deceptions,
tie up at the first port of call. Here.
We are owed a souvenir, an explanation.

# Clean Break

My teeth are a loom.  They clatter
as I look where the hand of the wind
bowled out the church roof.
Slates and lead lifted up
like a dustbin lid.  Villagers brood
six deep in the soil.
I tread on their inscriptions.

The hotel lounge is full
of well-intentioned women
exchanging recipes for hotpot.
A bearded man gets me chocolate.
One bar milk, one plain.  His thigh
edges mine on the sofa.  But I'm cold
as a chimney in the valley.

Unwritten postcards curl in my pocket.
Calling you from a phone box
would be trespass.  Like a touch
on the spine of someone sleeping near.
A walk across moorland
without boots or map or compass.
No love.  I can't wish you here.

# Hand in Glove

Time to run from her rich house
with its stacked towels and dizzy pillowcases.

From helpings of sweet unsalted food.
Nothing my incisors can chisel or tear.

Every night I am smothered by goosedown,
drowned in a bed I don't know how to share.

She has given me disguises: fine-knitted fabric
to muffle my big paws and broken nails.

She pets me too lightly, moves round me nervously.
We both understand I'm not domesticated.

That I need to curl up, reject, roll away,
hide in my own half-demolished spaces.

But when I step into the glassy coach
and she flaps a brave wing, I miss her.

When I'm shuttling down the motorway
or delayed in a vandal-proof shelter, I'm with her.

As a strange woman tries to make conversation
and the bus lumbers through drab estates, I love her.

Finding one pocket empty - her present's lost already,
I long to reverse my destination.

To ease my twitching arteries once more
inside her deep lambswool and angora.

# Marrow

**marrow, n.** *the soft tissue in the hollow parts of the bones: pith or pulp of plants (obs.): a vegetable marrow: the essence or best part of anything: the inner meaning or purpose.*
**marrow, (N.Eng. dial.) n.** *a mate: a companion: a match, equal, like: one of a pair.*

### 1

The morning off.  Under a clear sky
I check my cultivated garden.
Runner beans twirl up their tent of canes.
The soft fruit darkens in its cage.

Behind the brassy female flowers
the first swellings have appeared.
Gaudy-green courgettes.  Their seeded flesh
to be sliced thin and fried.

Only a chosen few making it
to marrow size.  High summer.
The strong plants kicking out
on a mad dash to the finish line.

I'd gone in to soap my hands.
After the glare, my kitchen was a cave
of strange dimensions.  I waited
for objects to come back into their places.

The bell rang.  Someone at the door.
This is nothing but the truth.
It lodges in my skull.
Just as 2 and 2 makes 4.

### 2

A social worker
from that place over the park.
We sit uncomfortably,
chairs not quite facing.

*It's about Vivien.*

- But Vivien's gone.
Two or three months back.
I turned the corner
and she disappeared into a cab
with all her stuff in rubbish bags.
A note on the table saying,
'Thank you very much.'
Nowhere to forward post.  No signature.
It must have been planned.

*She was referred to us in April.*
*Now I wonder.  Did Vivien mention family*
*to you?  An address?*
*Any scrap of information.*
*We'd be most grateful.*

- I only know there was a sister.

*Because we need to ask the next of kin*
*about arrangements.  Not to worry.*
*The police are sifting through her papers.*

She gets up.  I close towards her.

- Something's happened, hasn't it?
Tell me what's happened.

A cross winks at the woman's throat.
One of her nails is badly bitten.

# 3

*I'll have a lie in tomorrow.*
*Those were her words last night.*
*Don't expect me down in time*
*to do the kitchen floor.*

*Someone goes to wake her at 11*

*and is greeted by the smell of vomit.*
*Her face gapes from the corner.*
*On a narrow chest, ribs showing.*
*Not a pretty sight.*

# 4

The quiet type.
Kept herself to herself.
Isn't that what people say?

First thing she looked dreadful.
Pinched face and bags under her eyes.
Skin a bluish shade.

Yet she left for the language school
immaculate in her floating skirt,
white blouse and fragile shoes.

Straight after supper -
Ryvita, cottage cheese, tinned sardines
- she'd creep upstairs.

And I'd be sure to catch her
knowing she wouldn't open
to some well-meant question,

or an invitation to watch Eastenders.
In the same way I'd gently try
a bathroom door,

not wanting to startle
somebody naked and remote,
within touching distance.

Finally she'd get her hot water bottle
and hunch by the kettle.  Half past 8
on a mild spring evening.

I thought it was something physical.

# 5

Vacancy.
The mattress stripped,
one grey blanket exactly folded.
Desk, chair, all ready
for renting out
to the next friend of an acquaintance
at so many pounds per month
including electricity.

I'm tugging out drawers.
I stick my finger
down the crack by the wall,
and open the wardrobe
where two wire hangers clang
disturbed.

On the lookout for a button.
Or a ball of cotton wool.
An old biro.  Even a bus ticket
would do.  But no.
The girl has picked herself
clean as a bone.

Beyond me.

# 6

The training pool is 4ft 6 each end.
No one can get out of their depth.
A lifeguard waits in wrap-round pleats.
Accidents are not allowed.

The water is packed with bodies,
anonymous in numbered armbands.
Nylon suits and hair slicked back,
going through the appropriate gestures.

We are in league.  Good people
who obey the sign, 'Lengths Only'.
Labouring backwards and forwards
we look after ourselves, take care

to avoid collision.  Only give
the occasional grunt or sigh.
This morning I want out.  I need
to be on some God-forsaken beach

where I might shred off every stitch
and have the cold waves cradle me
then put me down on stone so sudden
I break my skin and bleed.  But I stay here

till my ears sing like a frenzied kettle.
All the time valves shut, re-open.
My heart nags on.
Its muscle does not fatigue.

# 7

Next to a friend's husband,
on our way to an expensive restaurant.

The broken hedges rushing past.
Sheep hurtle in reverse
as his fat voice blunders.
Tragedy.  Waste.  How shocked we were.

I imagine
he would be more shocked
if I sank my teeth into his arm,
or wrenched the steering wheel.

He goes crashing on.
If Vivien had been prescribed the right medication.
If she had been psycho-analysed.
Pay no attention.  Live and let live.

I shall sit with this man
at a starched table
and eat my fancy dinner.  Behaving nicely.
Making conversation.

He won't guess that there are trespasses
I can't forgive.

# 8

At first I couldn't tell
why the leaves went patchy.
A lack of minerals perhaps.

Then the fruits became misshapen.
It was mosaic virus
which had got into the cells

and multiplied.  There's no cure.
According to the book
affected plants should be destroyed.

Although I'm glutted
with buckets and boxes full of plums,
frilled lettuce, new potatoes;

although I've boiled and frozen,
packed cupboards with preserves
(each jar bearing its neat label),

this tearing up, the burning
of these flaccid bodies
grieves me far beyond proportion.

There could have been marrows,
shining, big and blatant.
Their tough skin a protection

for the gentle flesh inside.

# Jam Today

Our unemployed season.
You in a high rise.
Me round the bend
in my shortlife basement.
We skived off on our bikes,
forgot job applications.

Purple handed
with blackberries from the city graveyard.
Sorting through crates after market.
Over the garden wall
to nick late rhubarb,
vicious gooseberries,
apples no larger than new potatoes.

But we could have been other women,
wide-bosomed,
smelling of laundry and wax polish.
Children upstairs.
Somewhere a wireless playing
as we bustle
in unfitted kitchens.

Juggling recipes and quantities,
we cut the bad bits out,
squeezed lemon halves,
nipped to the shop
for one more bag of sugar.
Saucepans wobbled
as they reached a rolling boil.
Warm jars queued up
for completeness.

These days we are distant
and meet in restaurants.
I'm down to my last pot.
*Plum 91* in smeared italics.
A clear gold colour.
I lay it on thick,
talk with my mouth full
of your sweetness.

# Calling

Your first name, your last,
lay scratched over in my book.
Just like all the other removals.

Till I saw you at night
holding hands with a stranger.
You started to turn, say something.
I woke and remembered.

How you put your key in my purse,
came to water my ferns and violets,
drove to fetch me a day early.

Now I'm pacing the shallow pavements
of a town I never meant to live in.
An evangelist
who scans the faces of tall women.

You could have traded in your car by now,
had your hair re-styled,
even started a baby.

Maybe you will simply re-appear
in these shops at the proper season,
like tips of asparagus
or new potatoes.

Only I can't wait.
Cupping the breast of the payphone,
I want your lips so dangerous and near.

# Refrigerant

The tenancy agreement says, *No pets*,
and she's mislaid her lover.

But she's got something more reliable,
a big white box

that squats in one corner.
Every night its jaw swings open

as she gives it food -
six eggs, unfertilised.

Nothing bad can multiply
beneath its frosted collar.

While she dozes to TV drama
or clicks through a knitting pattern,

she's accompanied by its naps
and sudden quickenings

until the warmth is lost.
Behind a sealed front door, blood thickens.

# The Exercise

*We must love one another or die.*


He just arrived.  This unnatural boy.
This entire stranger
who is standing near enough to touch,
whose eyes embrace me.

I start to shed my clothes.
A cardigan with complicated buttons,
shirt cuffs, an awkward trouser zip,
unwanted underwear.  Material falsities

which thicken, tangle, multiply.
I anticipate the fine edge of his hips
dancing above me.  When our bodies collide
it should be terrifying.

I stumble trying to unpick
my double-knotted laces.
Not ready.  If I don't hurry
we shall miss our connection.


*We must love one another . . .*


My fingers are oiled with sweat.
I jerk and fumble.  My tongue is dumb.
Ears ring with noise
as I watch him.  He

is breaking up in front of me.
All these angles and surfaces of desire
disintegrate like glass in a kaleidoscope
before the twist of rearrangement.

A square mirror.  A gap between two curtains.
My mouth that's cracked and vacant.
He is no more solid
than my impulses can paint him.

I'll wake and walk the town,
go seek his figure or its closest imitation.
Then pull him into me.
Quickly.  Now.  Oh yes.


*We must love one another and die.*

# Carnivore

Cards lie in wait as bookmarks.
Your birthday looms from an unfilled page.

And I never met so many women
with a look of you - through car windows,

caught on sad photographs
at the turn of the library stair.

All the long passage of this year
no more than a little boy's touch.

Could I forget such hair,
dark angels on your body?

Your apple breath.
Your brazen kissing.

Why should I be woken by wrong numbers?
Each footstep nearing my door

makes me jerk like a phantom limb.
Now we are both disabled.

Do you still hunger to slice me open
like a breakfast egg?

Or take me apart as a crossword clue
for the attention of your lover?

Did you find it difficult
to winch my stump out of your garden?

If you should think to ask
my bulletin is simple.

*I got the offer of a well-paid job.*
*And I like to eat dead animals.*

# Psychic

The man in the maisonette
said *It's pressure - you not sharing my bed,*
*but I know it would be wrong to rape you.*
*Like stealing* he said.

She was frightened of the kitchen knife in the drawer.
The knob that might turn in the locked door.

Her mother sent her a postcard
of Indian erotic art.
That hand on a girl's round breast.
She tore the picture in half.

Her father sent a letter
saying *If you are in any kind of trouble.*
*If there's a way we can help.*

She gave no notice.
Took a bus to a seaside town.
Slept in a room with a Bible
and a shiny purple eiderdown,

She hadn't a clue about tomorrow.
But there was a sign,
*Fortunes Told This Way,*
so she followed the arrow.

The clairvoyant pocketed five pounds
and said *You're on the run*
*from a man with heavy eyes*
*who wants too much.*

All afternoon the tide pounded down and on.
*More than enough* it said.
*More than enough.*

# Halfway House

Morning is dreadful.
Mouth foggy with diazepam.
A slippy floor. Kitchen swarming
but no one picks up the phone.
The volunteer has roared away
with the vacuum cleaner.
All we can manage
is to reach the kettle and drop
our limp slices inside the toaster.

Not long back
we earned good wages,
paid the gas bill,
went to the gym midweek,
opened a bottle on Sundays,
Now bits of us are missing.
A colon. A uterus.
How to read a book
or get to the railway station.

We have new occupations.
A flip through mail-order fashion.
Hours on the quick crossword.
Consulting the telly page.
Once our lovers came.
They sat on the edge,
took in the vase of flowers
and heavy carpet,
the smell of polish and roast potatoes.
And they were full of admiration.

This year, next year,
the Officer-in-Charge will fetch us
for a chat with Matron and the doctor
about our progress.
They will halve our dosages
and design a programme of rehabilitation.
If someone would give us a key,
we could lock the red door
where faces appear without warning.
We want to stop here.

# Reasonable Hotel

She can pick up dangerous cutlery
quite safely now, enquire about ailments
or the choice of consumer durables.
They discuss planned holidays, redecoration.

Everything is swallowed eagerly.
Small talk and larger portions.
Piped music oozes round each pause,
sweetly bright as custard.

So why does she want to hook words
from her mouth's back corner?
To lay them on the separating cloth
like horrid lumps of gristle.

Tell them her pills have stopped working
and the doctor won't give anything stronger.
Say her walls are far too thin.
She's kept awake by the neighbours' quarrels.

That 39 people are after every vacancy
while she wastes hours along library shelves
or supermarket aisles, unable to fill
her basket. She feels so little.

If opportunity was offered, that time's passed.
Coffee is served in bitter baby cups.
They swear it's been lovely, but they're anxious
to get home before dark.

# A New Word

Today I learn a new word

after being trapped for years
in the limited vocabulary
of stiff-lipped
limp-pricked Englishmen
who are so furtively uncertain
they always have to check
the door is locked
before they cut the lights
and shut the curtain.
Who choose to use
such feeble phrases
like the verb
*to bonk*
as if we were characters in a comic
two-dimensional, absurd.

I plucked this word from another language.

It is a babble of consonants
an ocean's sibilance
hissing *yes*
as it crashes down on a coast of stone.
It is a litany of vowels
cool and sweet as citrus
fresh-squeezed on the tongue.
My lips pout and linger
over its diphthong.
It is much stronger
than that brief nervous spasm
*orgasm*
yet laden with nuance.
I'll keep this word
till someone pleads in my ear.
*Tell me. What do you want?*

My answer will be *jouissance*.

# Reader, Writer

I'm an amateur. One of many
to stay at a Welsh hotel, off-season.
The last group did Personal Growth.
This weekend it's Poetry.

You are our glitzy tutor.
Praised, prized, much-anthologised,
with your caseful of workshop tricks,
your cigarettes and feedback.

&ast;

I have turned to you;
tuning my radio to odd frequencies
in the middle of dry afternoons.
Or kept myself awake

for the taste of your malt whisky voice,
broadcasting intimacy.
You utter metaphors
that make the little hairs of my ears vibrate.

&ast;

Now you take the stage
of the town's smallest theatre,
A festival guest in half-rhymed clothes
and post-modern haircut.

I sit being wooed by your wit.
Each part of speech an occasion of lust.
Your lyrics like bites.
Or deliberate, slow kisses.

&ast;

I wait in line
as you sign copies of your new collection.
You forget how we met.
I must jog your memory.

Homebound on the long-winded bus,
I bend back the cover.
*Warm wishes* you scrawled on the page.
And my name spelled wrongly.

# KISS and TELL

The WINE is GONE
and TALK has COME to a STOP.
*MOVE OVER HERE*, SAYS the POET.
He PATS the SOFA.

His FACE is a brown SHOE
THAT has SEEN plenty of WEAR.
The ARCH of his NECK LIKE a CAT'S,
VERY NEAR.

But his tongue is a FISH on the SLAB
and his teeth HURT my LIPS.
My MIND GETS in a SPIN
as he RUBS his PALM across my TITS.

WILL someone WALK through the DOOR?
Is there a WIFE LEFT at HOME?
ALSO DOES he HAVE KIDS?
His HAND starts to PLAY between my LEGS.

WHEN my BODY begins to FEEL
LIKE a RUDE WORD on a WALL,
I WANT to HANG ONTO his HIPS
and HAVE it AWAY TILL DAWN.

ONLY he SAYS it is LATE
and GOES off.
Was it JUST a GOOD SNOG THEN,
nothing MORE?

SOON I SUSS it out.
Our LOVE GAVE him an IDEA.
He had to RUSH to his ROOM in TIME
to write it DOWN.

I shall STAR on EACH PAGE
of his NEXT BOOK.
HE'LL FIND out where I LIVE
and SEND me a FREE COPY.

Everyone in TOWN WILL READ it
and be DEAD KEEN to KNOW
the REAL NAME of THAT SEXY GIRL.
At LONG LAST FAME - WHAT LUCK!

# Protective

Just one night of skirmishes, incursions,
and you are ready to pull out
from our disputed border.
Go on home, regroup your forces.
No damage done, my intra-uterine device
was there to repel invaders.

You are so hasty in departure,
scattering hostages around my room.
Like your ragged scarf that smelled
of rain and bonfires.
A trophy I wore for several months
before it was recaptured.

Or dropping valuable intelligence
in my wastepaper bin.
We had stopped at the cashpoint
before a meal and mutual interrogation.
Smoothing the receipt I read with interest
how deep you were in credit.

Today's consolation prize is you
going off without your wallet.
I finger through its nearly female pockets.
Only a tenner and some plastic.
In the innermost fold, one sachet.
The rubber lip of it; a condom.

I can feel the split coming.
We are to become considerate,
speaking infrequently on the phone,
exchanging cards at Christmas.
When you rush back, flustered by loss,
I'll hand it all over. And kiss you.

# Unnatural History

You have chosen the past perfect.
This is why we visit worked-out quarries
disused Wesleyan chapels
and slagheaps,
travelling inland on single-track roads
to remote, intolerant valleys.

You tell me so proudly
these mean villages are the site
of a revolution that never quite happened.
They are your patch now,
places where you don't need a map
and can speak the language.

But at night beneath the nylon bedspread
of our boarding-house
you become a clumsy tourist
giving my body a quick once-over,
afraid of getting lost
down any of its bewildering alleys.

I insist on the simple present.
For our final day
we must go to the sea.
I rush across an alphabet of pebbles
bruising my tender feet
so fierce is my need to get

good salt-water that scours and erodes
every trace of evidence.
Already I'm up to my knees.
While you sit on a boulder
in your patent shoes and city jacket
studying the book I lent you - a Penguin Classic.

Not once thinking you might lift your eyes
to the half-naked kids
who squabble with buckets and cola cans
about your ankles,
look up to the dateless mountains
or my disappearing figure.

# Bad Trip

The bus circles past blue slate,
heaped rejects.  I've come too far
into her ugly village
where quarrymen's houses grip the valley.
The border signs read, *Welcome,*
but the spray paint said,
*Go home you English bastards.*

My lips press the letter box
shouting her name to no one.
I can see she's been busy
knocking down walls, spending a packet
on Swedish pine.  What has she done
to the damp back bedroom
in which we held each other?

She would be in the hotel,
Martini in hand, trying out new phrases
on the old boys in the corner.
When the singing's over
she must come back to find me
curled in the porch,
picking dry petals off her geranium.

I was never the one she expected.

# Curriculum Vitae

Suddenly aged 33.  Single.
Looking at a man
who could be my father.

I'm one of an assortment
sent by the Benefit Office.
His job is to help us get jobs.
He's ex-army,
spent years in recruitment.

In the morning
he describes the ideal pattern of employment
going steadily up.
On his blue tie a deployment
of fighter planes
rises in strict progression.

After lunch we write CVs
and have private interviews.
My defences polished like his shoes,
I enter first
with one and a half pages of selected truth;
personal details, the passable education,
an implausible work history.
Gaps interrupt his splayed-out teeth.

I may have stretched the fabric
of what happened -
false starts, a stopping short,
- to the limit.
He has a girl's small breasts
and neat round gut
beneath his polycotton shirt.

His eyes commute
from the lines arranged as carefully
as he has combed his fading hair,
to my sharp expression.
He puts one question,

*Something went wrong didn't it?*
And I shiver.
It feels like undressing

# Nothing Personal

Come and gone
from my snug pigeonhole.
He's in the bath.

My fingerprints, our kisses
flaking off.
They will dry to a grey circle.

Now his plump skin
has been checked in cotton,
buttoned up in tweed.

We peck on the chilly step.
Until next time then.
A sleek car nosing into traffic.

Daylight winks at me
as I pick up
the single pint of milk.

*IRON Press was formed in Spring 1973, initially to publish the magazine IRON which more than two decades, and more than 1,500 writers on, survives as one of the country's most active alternative mags – a fervent purveyor of new poetry, fiction and graphics. £12.00 gets you a subscription. Try our intriguing book list too, titles which can rarely be found on the shelves of mega-stores. Fortified by a belief in good writing, as against literary competitions or marketing trivia, IRON remains defiantly a small press. Our address is at the front of this book*